Up and Off!

Written by Karra McFarlane

Collins

It can go up.

It tips up and off.

Bill gets the ill man.

The man can go up.

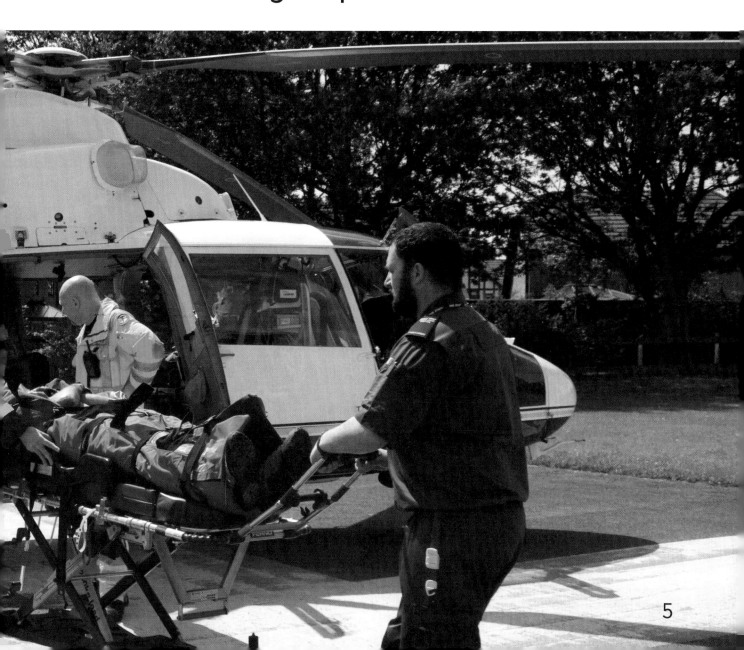

It can go on up.

It tips up and off.

Lin can not miss Fin.

Lin can pick Fin up.

It can go on up.

It tips up and off.

Len gets the big dog.

The big dog licks Len.

SS

14

15

🐾 Review: After reading 🐾

Use your assessment from hearing the children read to choose any GPCs, words or tricky words that need additional practice.

Read 1: Decoding
- Turn to page 3. Say the word **tips**. Ask the children if they can sound out each of the letter sounds in the word **tips** and then blend them. (*t/i/p/s* – **tips**)
- Ask the children if they can think of any words that rhyme with **tips**. (e.g. *dips, sips, skips*)
- Look at the "I spy sounds" pages (14–15). Say the sounds together. How many items can the children spot that have the /f/ sound in them (e.g. *fish, factory, flippers, starfish*) or "ss" in them? (e.g. *grass, dress*)

Read 2: Prosody
- Model reading each page with expression to the children. After you have read each page, ask the children to have a go at reading with expression.

Read 3: Comprehension
- For every question ask the children how they know the answer. Ask:
  - Can you remember how helicopters were used in the book? (*to rescue an ill person, to pick up a person from the sea and to rescue a dog*)
  - How was the person rescued from the sea? (*using a rope*)
  - Why do you think the people in the book would use a helicopter to rescue people instead of a car? (*they are quicker, they can reach difficult places*)
  - Would you like to go in a helicopter? Why or why not?